T0353212

STEPHANIE JACOB

Stephanie Jacob is a writer and actor.

Her first play, *Harry's Window*, about sibling rivalry among the over-eighties, had readings at the New Ambassadors, Soho Theatre and the National Theatre Studio, where Stephanie has subsequently been a Writer-on-Attachment.

The Quick, about restorative justice, was produced at the Tristan Bates Theatre, London, and was Time Out Critics' Choice for its run ('a tough and touching new play... fitting wit into the anguish... ever more tender' *Time Out*; 'clever and sharp, not easy to watch but very rewarding viewing' *A Younger Theatre*).

Her radio play, *A Night Visitor*, about a transformative pig (BBC Radio 4 Afternoon Drama), won the Writers' Guild Best Radio Drama Award.

The Strongbox premiered at VAULT Festival 2018.

As an actor, Stephanie has worked at the National Theatre, RSC, in repertory, touring theatre and in the West End.

Mike Bartlett
ALBION
BULL
GAME
AN INTERVENTION
KING CHARLES III
WILD

Jez Butterworth
THE FERRYMAN
JERUSALEM
JEZ BUTTERWORTH PLAYS: ONE
MOJO
THE NIGHT HERON
PARLOUR SONG
THE RIVER
THE WINTERLING

Caryl Churchill
BLUE HEART
CHURCHILL PLAYS: THREE
CHURCHILL PLAYS: FOUR
CHURCHILL: SHORTS
CLOUD NINE
DING DONG THE WICKED
A DREAM PLAY *after* Strindberg
DRUNK ENOUGH TO SAY
    I LOVE YOU?
ESCAPED ALONE
FAR AWAY
HERE WE GO
HOTEL
ICECREAM
LIGHT SHINING IN
    BUCKINGHAMSHIRE
LOVE AND INFORMATION
MAD FOREST
A NUMBER
PIGS AND DOGS
SEVEN JEWISH CHILDREN
THE SKRIKER
THIS IS A CHAIR
THYESTES *after* Seneca
TRAPS

Phil Davies
FIREBIRD

debbie tucker green
BORN BAD
DIRTY BUTTERFLY
HANG
NUT
A PROFOUNDLY AFFECTIONATE,
    PASSIONATE DEVOTION TO
    SOMEONE (– *NOUN*)
RANDOM
STONING MARY
TRADE & GENERATIONS
TRUTH AND RECONCILIATION

Matt Hartley
DEPOSIT
HERE I BELONG
MICROCOSM
SIXTY FIVE MILES

Rose Heiney
ELEPHANTS

Sam Holcroft
COCKROACH
DANCING BEARS
EDGAR & ANNABEL
PINK
RULES FOR LIVING
THE WARDROBE
WHILE YOU LIE

Stephanie Jacob
THE STRONGBOX

Vicky Jones
THE ONE
TOUCH

Anna Jordan
CHICKEN SHOP
FREAK
YEN

Andrew Keatley
ALLIGATORS
THE GATHERED LEAVES

Lucy Kirkwood
BEAUTY AND THE BEAST
    with Katie Mitchell
BLOODY WIMMIN
THE CHILDREN
CHIMERICA
HEDDA *after* Ibsen
IT FELT EMPTY WHEN THE HEART
    WENT AT FIRST BUT IT IS
    ALRIGHT NOW
LUCY KIRKWOOD PLAYS: ONE
MOSQUITOES
NSFW
TINDERBOX

Sam Potter
HANNA

Katherine Soper
WISH LIST

Jack Thorne
2ND MAY 1997
A CHRISTMAS CAROL *after* Dickens
BUNNY
BURYING YOUR BROTHER
    IN THE PAVEMENT
HOPE
JACK THORNE PLAYS: ONE
JUNKYARD
LET THE RIGHT ONE IN
    after John Ajvide Lindqvist
MYDIDAE
STACY & FANNY AND FAGGOT
WHEN YOU CURE ME
WOYZECK *after* Büchner

Phoebe Waller-Bridge
FLEABAG

Tom Wells
BROKEN BISCUITS
FOLK
JUMPERS FOR GOALPOSTS
THE KITCHEN SINK
ME, AS A PENGUIN

Stephanie Jacob

AGAIN

NICK HERN BOOKS

London

www.nickhernbooks.co.uk

A Nick Hern Book

Again first published in Great Britain as a paperback original in 2018
by Nick Hern Books Limited, The Glasshouse, 49a Goldhawk Road,
London W12 8QP

Again copyright © 2018 Stephanie Jacob

Stephanie Jacob has asserted her right to be identified as the author of this work

Cover image: Rebecca Pitt

Designed and typeset by Nick Hern Books, London
Printed in the UK by Mimeo Ltd, Huntingdon, Cambridgeshire PE29 6XX

A CIP catalogue record for this book is available from the British Library

ISBN 978 1 84842 746 4

Woodland
CARBON
www.woodlandcarbon.co.uk
NICK HERN BOOKS
Printed on Carbon Captured paper

Again was first performed at Trafalgar Studios 2, London, on 6 February 2018, with the following cast:

TOM	Chris Larkin
LOUISE	Natasha Little
ADAM	Charles Reston
IZZY	Rosie Day

Director	Hannah Price
Designer	Anthony Lamble
Lighting Designer	Sally Ferguson
Sound Designer	Seb Frost
Movement	Gillian Reston
Producers	Mongrel Thumb

Characters

TOM, *a builder, fifty-four*
LOUISE, *his ex-wife, a book editor, fifty-two*
ADAM, *their son, a PhD student, twenty-five*
IZZY, *their daughter, between jobs, twenty-three*

Note on Play

The action is set now in a house in south-east London.

Each character has a chair.

If they want to restart the action, they reset their chair.

If they're outside, they sit and remain visible to other characters.

Speech in brackets indicates a private thought.

This text went to press before the end of rehearsals and so may differ slightly from the play as performed.

ARRIVAL

TOM *comes*.

LOUISE. Don't stand there, give me your –

TOM. I'll keep it on just now.

LOUISE. Okay.

They look at each other.

Adam's on his way.

TOM. What, now?

LOUISE. He's walking up from the station.

TOM. I thought I was early.

LOUISE. You are.

TOM. Look. Before he gets here. But you're not going to like it.

LOUISE. Keep an open mind.

TOM. Eh?

LOUISE. I'm just saying. Am I so predictable?

TOM. Yep.

LOUISE. Thanks.

TOM. You always –

LOUISE. Well, there's always something, Tom, something always crops up that makes everything impossible –

TOM. That's not fair!

LOUISE. No.

TOM. What?

LOUISE. It isn't. Fuck. Sorry.

LOUISE *resets her chair*.

LOUISE. Adam's on his way.

TOM. What, now?

LOUISE. He's walking up from the station.

TOM. Shit.

LOUISE. You said the money was sorted.

TOM. No, it is.

LOUISE. Okay, good.

TOM. It is and it isn't.

LOUISE. Oh Tom, please –

TOM. Listen, no, just something else has come up –

LOUISE. Don't do this!

TOM. I'm not doing anything –

LOUISE. Yes because you won't put them first, *our children* you won't put first in your long, long list of –

TOM. I work, that's all I do, work and work and work, I'm going to work till I drop dead, Louise, and as I fall to the ground I'm going to think that was *it*?

LOUISE. Whose fault is that?

TOM. Mine! All of it, everything's –

LOUISE. Fuck.

TOM. What?

LOUISE. Sorry. Sorry sorry sorry. I didn't mean to do that.

TOM. Okay.

LOUISE. I meant *not* to do that, I meant to be all cool and letting things go and – but when we start I just –

TOM. I know.

LOUISE. Yeah.

TOM. Yeah.

LOUISE. I try for Yoda, it comes out Margaret Thatcher.

TOM *laughs*.

Go on. Before Adam gets here.

TOM. How is he?

LOUISE. Good, I think. You know what he's like.

TOM. Cards close to his chest.

LOUISE. He'd make a great spy.

TOM. Maybe he is one.

LOUISE *laughs*.

Maybe he's bugged the house.

LOUISE. I worry about it, you know, if he's a bit closed off?

TOM. With you?

LOUISE. Secretive. And Izzy, running from one mess to another mess –

TOM. She's twenty-three.

LOUISE. Is it us, though?

TOM. What?

LOUISE. Have we done it to them?

TOM. Cos of breaking up, you mean? I don't see that. Ad was always, he'd slip off your lap, you'd find him reading somewhere, a loner, I suppose –

LOUISE. This is different.

TOM. Izzy was always off on her little scooter, no, I think they're there from the beginning, look at Chloe, she's five, I can already see exactly who she's going to be.

LOUISE. Who?

TOM. A nurse or a teacher or some poor harassed social worker, she's desperate for a pet now, we can't have pets in the flat.

LOUISE. What about a secret hamster?

TOM. She's scared of hamsters.

LOUISE. Izzy was!

TOM. Too bitey.

LOUISE. D'you think they're happy?

TOM. Chloe is.

LOUISE. Ours, I mean.

TOM. Happy. But who is?

LOUISE. I think we should help them be happy.

TOM. Course.

LOUISE. Try, anyway.

TOM. Course we should.

LOUISE. Yeah? Okay, then.

TOM. What have I just agreed to?

They look at each other.

TOM *resets his chair.*

LOUISE. Adam's on his way.

TOM. What, now?

LOUISE. He's walking up from the station.

TOM. Right.

LOUISE. What?

TOM. Well, let's have a beer.

LOUISE. I don't drink beer, remember?

TOM. Glass of wine, then. Quick catch-up, come on.

LOUISE. Is it the money?

TOM. For God's sake, Louise, can't we just –

LOUISE. Is it, though?

TOM. Why would you think –

LOUISE. Because you're always flaky about money.

TOM. Unbelievable.

ADAM. Mum?

ADAM *comes*.

I brought a pineapple!

ADAM *hugs* LOUISE.

Everyone likes pineapple, don't they?

TOM. Can we have it on sticks?

ADAM. Oh.

TOM. You didn't know I was coming.

ADAM. No.

LOUISE. Izzy says she's on her way.

ADAM. You said it was just us.

LOUISE. It is.

ADAM. We're allowed to make choices, you know.

LOUISE. If I'd said Dad was coming –

ADAM. Yes. You should've.

LOUISE. Adam. Please?

ADAM. Sorry.

ADAM *leaves*.

LOUISE. Fuck.

TOM. Why didn't you tell him?

LOUISE. He wouldn't have come.

TOM. That makes me feel so good about myself.

LOUISE. No, no, it's not you, it's the whole thing.

TOM. Yeah?

TOM *resets his chair*.

ADAM. I brought a pineapple!

   ADAM *hugs* LOUISE.

   Everyone likes pineapple, don't they?

TOM. Can we have it on sticks?

ADAM. Oh.

TOM. You didn't know I was coming.

ADAM. No.

LOUISE. Izzy says she's on her way.

ADAM. I once waited two-and-a-half hours for that girl.

TOM. Gallant of you.

ADAM. I was in a pub with John Keats, so I was alright.

TOM. With who?

ADAM. John Keats?

TOM. Did I meet him? Was he at school with you?

ADAM. The poet? 'Beauty is truth, truth beauty'?

TOM. Right.

ADAM. 'Season of mists and mellow – '

TOM. Ah! Gotcha.

ADAM. Planning a quick getaway, Dad?

TOM. Eh?

ADAM. Coat.

   TOM *laughs*.

TOM. You get that job?

ADAM. Yeah.

TOM. Yeah?

ADAM. But the teaching's only two days a week, so Mum's going to let me live here pretty much for free –

TOM. So I hear, good plan. And you're carrying on with the – poetry thing?

ADAM. Extraordinary, isn't it?

TOM. It is a bit, if I'm honest.

They laugh.

And Helen?

ADAM. She's off to Bristol soon to do her postdoc.

TOM. Great girl.

ADAM. She is as it goes, but how you could possibly know what kind of girl – I mean you've met her once, Dad, and you stood there like a mute. That came out weirdly.

TOM. S'okay.

ADAM. Look, I'll just –

LOUISE. Adam! Please?

ADAM. Garden, Mum. Ciggie.

LOUISE. Oh.

ADAM. Relax.

ADAM sits, rolls a cigarette.

TOM. 'No, no, it's not you, it's the whole thing.'

LOUISE. It is! He finds it sort of intolerable.

TOM. Then why do you keep on with it?

LOUISE. Because.

They look at each other.

They watch ADAM.

TOM. So he smokes now?

LOUISE. Seems to. Helen smokes.

TOM. Do you still?

LOUISE. On and off. Apparently it's not very good for you.

TOM. Shall I go?

LOUISE. No.

TOM. I'll go.

LOUISE. Tom. Just give him a minute.

TOM. You've been digging.

LOUISE. Mulching.

TOM. You've been busy.

LOUISE. The garden's busy. Loads of frogspawn this year.

TOM. You've taken the old rose out.

LOUISE. And the apple tree's got to go.

TOM. No! It was here when we got here.

LOUISE. I know. I'll plant another one.

TOM. It won't be the same.

LOUISE. But that's alright, isn't it? Anyway, I think it's nearly finished.

TOM. The garden?

LOUISE. Mm.

TOM. You said a garden's never finished.

LOUISE. Did I?

TOM *resets his chair.*

ADAM. I brought a pineapple!

    ADAM *hugs* LOUISE.

    Everyone likes pineapple, don't they?

TOM. And I've got beers in the car.

ADAM. Hi, Dad.

TOM. Fancy one?

ADAM. I'm alright.

TOM. Crisps? I've got plain or cheese and onion.

ADAM. I'm alright, thanks.

TOM. How's things?

ADAM. Yeah. You?

TOM. Yeah, yeah.

Silence.

ADAM *and* LOUISE *talk to themselves at the same time, but in their own rhythm*:

LOUISE. go on push, wade through it, okay it feels horrible, but do it, look at him, let him look into your eyes

ADAM. every time you do this, bring him, let's be friends, every time this forced, lame, why keep on with it?

Silence.

TOM. I'll bring them in anyway, shall I?

ADAM. I don't want crisps, for God's sake!

TOM. Right.

ADAM. Right.

TOM. Bag of pork scratchings?

ADAM *laughs.*

IZZY. Mum?

IZZY *comes.*

Sorry I'm –

LOUISE. Phone! Why can't you phone?

IZZY. Well, I'm here now.

IZZY *hugs* LOUISE.

Anyway I couldn't.

LOUISE. Why?

IZZY. I'm not totally sure where my phone is.

LOUISE. Izzy.

IZZY (*hugging* ADAM). I think I left it at the party.

LOUISE. I am not repeat not buying you another one.

IZZY. Hi, Dad.

TOM. Your hair.

IZZY. It's my Heidi look, what d'you think?

TOM. It'll grow on me.

TOM/IZZY. Ha-ha.

ADAM. And where have you left your sheep?

IZZY. Goats. Heidi had goats.

ADAM. Sheep.

IZZY. Mum?

LOUISE. Heidi had goats.

ADAM. Stupid girls' book.

LOUISE. Does Boyd like it?

IZZY. Oh, Boyd.

LOUISE. (Round.)

TOM. (Muddy.)

ADAM. (Singing.)

IZZY. Maybe my phone's at his.

LOUISE. But you just came from his.

IZZY. He wouldn't let me in.

LOUISE. What?

IZZY. I know! So childish.

ADAM. What have you done?

IZZY. Nothing.

ADAM. Boyd, my poor friend.

IZZY. He wouldn't come to the party last night, when I got back this morning he wouldn't let me in.

LOUISE. You stayed over?

IZZY. He's sulking.

ADAM. He is a formidable sulker.

IZZY. I stood in the street and sang him a song, he still wouldn't.

TOM. What was the song?

IZZY (*sings*). Boyd, Boyd, I know you're annoyed, remember the sweet nights we've enjoyed, you think with your feelings I may have toyed, but this business would interest Sigmund Freud.

They all laugh.

(*Bowing.*) I thank you.

ADAM. God, your life.

IZZY. What about it?

ADAM *resets his chair.*

LOUISE. Phone! Why can't you phone?

IZZY. Well, I'm here now.

IZZY *hugs* LOUISE.

LOUISE. Lunch is ruined.

IZZY. We woke up madly late, it's Boyd's fault.

LOUISE. It's a blackened wreck.

IZZY. Too late for the bus.

LOUISE. So phone!

IZZY. I know.

LOUISE. But you didn't.

IZZY. I know!

LOUISE. But why?

IZZY. I'm telling you! So I need a cab but I've got no cash, so I run to the corner shop for cash, I get in the cab, I think must phone Mum and can you believe it?

ADAM. So easily.

IZZY. I've left my phone in the shop.

They all laugh.

TOM. Your hair.

IZZY. Is it a bit Miss Marple?

TOM. It'll grow on me.

TOM/IZZY. Ha-ha.

IZZY. I'm going to bleach it, Mum.

LOUISE. As long as it's not blue.

TOM. It was blue?

LOUISE. She looked like a Smurf.

ADAM. I told you, they have blue faces, not blue hair. She looked like a troll.

TOM. I'm sorry I missed that one.

IZZY (*hugging* ADAM). Boyd hated it, too. Poor Boyd.

LOUISE. (Sandwiches.)

TOM. (Boots.)

TOM/ADAM. (Collarbone.)

IZZY. He said to say sorry, we were up all night, well, he was, I kept falling asleep.

ADAM. What have you done?

IZZY. Nothing.

LOUISE. He's not ill?

IZZY. He kept going over and over everything.

ADAM. Ugh.

IZZY. Totally. (*To* LOUISE.) Don't look like that. It was just sex.

LOUISE. There's no such thing.

IZZY. It's allowed, he knows that, he agrees to it, then, I dunno, he gets sort of –

LOUISE. Hurt?

IZZY. He like bubbles up.

ADAM. He's mad to have anything to do with you.

IZZY. I keep telling him.

ADAM. So do I.

IZZY. Then I couldn't wake up this morning.

ADAM. So because of your riotous sex life we have to starve?

IZZY. Shall I knock us up an omelette?

LOUISE/TOM/ADAM. No!

ADAM. You can't cook, remember?

TOM. Eggsactly.

IZZY. Charming.

ADAM. God, your life.

IZZY. What about it?

ADAM *resets his chair.*

IZZY. Well, I'm here now.

    IZZY *hugs* LOUISE.

ADAM. Oh my God. You're actually here.

LOUISE. Izzy!

IZZY. Impressed?

LOUISE. Astounded.

IZZY. Am I early? I think I'm –

ADAM. One minute late, which in your case is effectively – oh God, let's call it early.

LOUISE. Let's! You Olympian.

IZZY (*bowing*). I thank you.

ADAM. What have you done?

IZZY. Nothing. I thought I'd help get lunch.

They all laugh.

That's not funny. Why's that funny?

LOUISE. Sweetheart. It's just –

IZZY. I do help.

LOUISE. You do.

IZZY. So why laugh?

ADAM. You're comical.

IZZY. Don't laugh.

ADAM. Then don't be comical.

IZZY. You have to make me seem like a hopeless case.

ADAM. *Seem* like one?

LOUISE. Adam.

ADAM. Oh come on, Mum, she's –

LOUISE. How's Boyd?

IZZY. It's better than sitting on the edge, like the boy who can't get in the pool.

LOUISE. I thought he was coming with you today?

IZZY. We've finished.

LOUISE. Izzy!

ADAM. You're not honestly surprised?

LOUISE. What happened?

IZZY. We got to the end. People do, it's not a tragedy, Mum. It was never a major thing, except in your head.

ADAM. And maybe Boyd's.

LOUISE. It's what you both want?

IZZY. Stop now or you'll make yourself miserable.

LOUISE. Well, I'm ever so sorry. I've always liked Boyd, ever
since Adam first met him, such a kind boy and he's –

IZZY. You go out with him, then!

TOM. Gently.

IZZY. Well, it's about time, isn't it?

LOUISE. Probably.

ADAM. At least he can scrub her out of his head now. (*To*
LOUISE.) No, Boyd's my friend, she's made him miserable
for months and months, he keeps trying to make sense of it
all, but there's no sense in what she does, just a horrible
heartless dance.

IZZY. I've left my bag there.

ADAM. What?

IZZY. I just left everything and ran. I'll have to go back and see
his face.

ADAM. Good.

LOUISE. Adam.

IZZY. His poor face.

LOUISE. (Eyebrows.)

ADAM. (Honest.)

TOM. (Blue.)

    IZZY *sobs.*

    LOUISE *moves towards her.*

IZZY. Don't.

    They watch IZZY *cry.*

    TOM *hands her his handkerchief.*

    (*Crying harder.*) Oh, Dad!

TOM. What?

IZZY. You're the only person in the world with a proper hankie!

TOM. What did the grape say when it was crushed?

IZZY (*handing back his hankie*). It let out a little wine.

TOM. Yup.

TABLE

Together they bring on a large wooden table.

TOM *strokes the wood.*

TOM. You haven't waxed it.

LOUISE. What?

TOM. Where's the wax?

LOUISE. I've had other things to think about.

TOM. The wood gets parched, that's all.

LOUISE. I've just been made redundant, Tom.

TOM. Still in the old place?

LOUISE. It's lunch in a minute.

TOM. I'll be two ticks.

TOM *leaves.*

ADAM (*quietly*). Did you know he was coming?

IZZY. Where's he gone?

ADAM. Iz!

IZZY. Course.

ADAM. So why am I the only one who –

LOUISE. Sssh!

IZZY. Cos you wouldn't come.

ADAM. Would.

IZZY. Wouldn't. You'd be sick.

ADAM. Wouldn't.

IZZY. Would. You'd have an emergency lecture to write.

ADAM. So instead of telling me, you trick me into –

LOUISE. Dad's finding this hard, too.

ADAM/IZZY. Good.

LOUISE. So can you be careful, please?

IZZY. No one mentioned careful.

LOUISE. Kind, try and be kind.

IZZY. I didn't say a thing.

ADAM (*to* LOUISE). What about you?

IZZY. What did I say?

ADAM. Do you have to be kind or just devious?

LOUISE. All of us try.

    TOM *comes with a suitcase.*

TOM. Try what?

LOUISE. That old thing!

TOM. Yep.

LOUISE. It'll be covered in dust.

TOM. I just cleaned it.

LOUISE. But what about lunch?

TOM. I'll be two ticks.

LOUISE. Fuck's sake, Tom.

TOM. Shall I not?

IZZY. She's just nervous in case it all goes to shit and Adam bolts again.

LOUISE. Izzy!

ADAM. I'm not a horse.

IZZY (*to* LOUISE). Well, aren't you?

LOUISE. Alright, yes!

IZZY (*waggling her fingers at* ADAM). Stay! Stay! Magic
Fingers, make him stay!

They all laugh.

TOM *opens the suitcase, takes out a cloth and a tin of wax.*

He opens the tin.

Oooh!

LOUISE. Mmm. I love that smell.

IZZY. What was that museum?

ADAM. From school?

IZZY. The one with the seahorses.

ADAM. Dead?

IZZY. Gliding.

ADAM. Oh. The Horniman.

IZZY. Yes.

TOM starts to polish the table, still in his coat.

LOUISE and IZZY watch.

ADAM takes a book out of the suitcase and reads, standing.

LOUISE. Well, they wouldn't chuck it out these days.

ADAM (*reading*). Who chucked it?

TOM. Builders. Top of the road.

LOUISE. An old lady'd lived there for years, they were ripping
everything out –

TOM. The fools.

LOUISE takes a cloth out of the suitcase and polishes.

*IZZY takes the suitcase and starts to look through it on
the floor.*

LOUISE. They just threw it in the skip, didn't they?

TOM. Yep.

LOUISE. I ran home, grabbed Dad, you were in your high
chair, we lugged it back here, then it sat in the front room –

ADAM. When it was still a wardrobe?

LOUISE. For months and months, all bashed up, till Dad took
it apart.

ADAM. Are we eating?

LOUISE. Soon.

ADAM. I'm starving.

IZZY. Help, then.

ADAM (*with distaste*). Sticky.

ADAM *reads, perching in various places.*

IZZY *takes the suitcase under the table.*

TOM. You never would get dirty.

LOUISE. Izzy used to eat dirt.

IZZY. Eat it?

TOM. Once she did.

LOUISE. We came back and found you lying in the flowerbed
like a slug.

IZZY. *What?*

They all laugh.

I do not look like a –

ADAM (*reading*). Do.

IZZY. Do not.

ADAM. One of those fat frilly orange ones.

IZZY. I do not –

ADAM. You so do.

LOUISE. Adam.

LOUISE *walks round the table, watching her family.*

IZZY *softly sing-talks under her breath.*

TOM (*polishing*). Where do sheep go on holiday?

ADAM (*reading*). The Baa-haa-mas. What did one wall say to the other?

TOM. Meet you at the corner. What does E.T. stand for?

ADAM. Um. Dunno.

TOM. Someone took his chair.

ADAM *laughs.*

LOUISE *puts her arms round* TOM *from behind.*

Do you want this done or not?

They kiss.

TOM *polishes.*

LOUISE *walks round the table and returns to polishing.*

IZZY *comes out with the suitcase.*

IZZY. So. Dad.

TOM. Izzy.

IZZY. Are we on? Are you subbing me on my project? Cos they can't pay me a bean.

LOUISE. Not even your air fare?

IZZY. And I want to go for six months.

LOUISE. Izzy!

IZZY. I told you that.

LOUISE. But I can't even Skype you there –

IZZY. When I'm in town you can. Come and stay!

ADAM. Is this for real? The nearest wifi's twenty miles away.

IZZY. I know, I'll be in heaven. No phone!

ADAM. You'll be desolate.

IZZY. D'you think I'm mad?

ADAM. Always.

IZZY. And they sing about everything! There's loads of hymns and praise, I think those are my favourite bits. Actually maybe I'm going cos it's like being in a musical.

LOUISE. Do am-dram instead.

IZZY. I'm going, Mum, for definite. If Dad can sub me.

The sound of TOM *polishing intently.*

LOUISE. Tom?

IZZY. Dad?

LOUISE. You said it was sorted.

IZZY. Mum can't help right now or I wouldn't ask.

TOM. Always ask.

LOUISE. Oh God, here we go.

IZZY. You promised.

TOM. No, it's not, well, it is about money, yes, but it's –

IZZY. Why do you do this?

TOM. Sweetheart –

LOUISE. Flaky.

IZZY. It's cruel.

TOM. No no!

LOUISE. It is.

IZZY. Why get my hopes up if you can't –

TOM. I'm not saying –

IZZY. Yes when you mean no –

TOM. Not no, no, but –

LOUISE. Fatally flaky.

TOM. Sheena's pregnant.

Silence.

IZZY. She must have a sixth sense.

ADAM. Iz.

IZZY. How else does she do it?

TOM. Sheena's –

IZZY. (Nails.)

ADAM. (Flirty.)

IZZY. (Quick.)

ADAM. (Unnerving.)

IZZY/ADAM/LOUISE. (Blonde.)

TOM. It's not like that.

IZZY. Every time!

ADAM. You're being a dick.

IZZY. Someone else in the family needs your help, she's like a dog, she gets wind of it and slips in ahead. We are still family, are we, Adam and me?

ADAM. A total dick.

IZZY. But it's so unfair!

ADAM *resets his chair.*

TOM. I'm not saying –

IZZY. Yes when you mean no –

TOM. Not no, no, but –

LOUISE. Fatally flaky.

TOM. Sheena's pregnant.

Silence.

LOUISE. I thought you'd stopped trying.

TOM. Yep.

LOUISE. You'd decided enough was enough.

TOM. It seems not.

LOUISE. Oh for God's sake.

TOM. What?

LOUISE. As if it's not your decision, too.

TOM. Well, it's not, really.

LOUISE. Immaculate conception, was it?

ADAM *laughs, shuts himself up.*

Things always just happen to you, don't they?

IZZY. Mum –

LOUISE. Everyone else can deal with the fallout.

TOM. That isn't fair.

IZZY. Try and be kind, you said.

LOUISE. I know! I'm sick of trying! Already! People don't even notice, they eat it up as if it's their just deserts. When it isn't. It really isn't.

TOM. If you saw her.

ADAM. (Lipstick.)

IZZY. (Zips.)

LOUISE. (Hair.)

TOM. She's so. Grieved about it all. I can't stand in her way.

LOUISE. Stupid cow.

ADAM/IZZY. Mum!

LOUISE. Me. I mean me!

LOUISE *resets her chair*.

TOM. I'm not saying –

IZZY. Yes when you mean no –

TOM. Not no, no, but –

LOUISE. Fatally flaky.

TOM. Sheena's pregnant.

Silence.

LOUISE. How far on is she?

TOM. Nearly four months. And she's sick as a parrot this time, remember how sick she was with Chloe?

IZZY. (Pale.)

ADAM. (Clever.)

LOUISE. (Worshipful.)

TOM. So she thinks it's a sign. That this one.

LOUISE. Will hang on in there.

TOM. Who knows?

LOUISE. That's a hard kind of waiting, Tom.

TOM. I can't really think about it.

LOUISE. No.

TOM. So if the baby. If she makes it –

LOUISE. It's a girl?

TOM. Yeah, we saw her on the.

IZZY. Dad.

TOM. See, Sheena can't work and the flat will be impossible, we're bursting at the seams as it is, so every bit of spare will have to go to finding somewhere bigger and –

IZZY. S'okay.

TOM. Oh, Iz.

IZZY. I get it.

TOM *polishes.*

Then LOUISE *polishes.*

Then IZZY *polishes.*

ADAM. Are we eating?

LOUISE. Soon.

ADAM. I'm starving.

IZZY. Help then.

ADAM *perches and reads.*

What did one flea say to the other?

LOUISE/TOM/ADAM. Shall we walk or take the dog?

HOUSE

LOUISE. How much do you want to go?

IZZY. Where?

LOUISE. The ends of the earth.

IZZY. A hundred and ten per cent. I think it might fix me.

LOUISE. You don't need fixing.

IZZY. You know what I mean.

LOUISE. Go on.

IZZY. Okay. So. (*To* ADAM.) Shut up.

ADAM. I'm reading.

IZZY. Well, keep reading.

ADAM. Did I say a word?

IZZY. So just don't. They walk for miles to come to school,
they're so like hungry thirsty for all the things I don't even

notice, they want to know everything, they make me happy and humble and ashamed all in one go, I think they'll make me saner or something, don't laugh, I mean like get a handle on what matters. You know?

LOUISE. Then what if I sell the house?

ADAM. You're not serious?

LOUISE. It just occurred to me.

Silence.

TOM, ADAM, IZZY *talk to themselves at the same time, but in their own rhythm:*

TOM. soon as she said that about the garden I knew she was, oh she's starting to leave which is, how many times have I wished she was, now it's here, I don't

ADAM. it's the house, you can't sell the house, we're not finished, there's stuff in here things that need, loads of stuff I'm not leaving till things are not finished

IZZY. is it? what is she? cos she's flushed and her eyes are all, I think she's like, oh my days she's starting to change things, yeah yeah and change

Silence.

ADAM. I don't think it's a good idea.

LOUISE. If I downsize to a flat, there'd still be a spare room for you, Ad, and I can give you both a lump sum –

ADAM. It doesn't make sense.

IZZY. Yes it does, yes yes yes, why doesn't it?

ADAM. Ask the estate agent in your bed.

LOUISE. Oh, d'you think Boyd would help us?

IZZY. To sell it? He'd love that!

ADAM. A London house! It's the one thing you've got that's a real investment, Mum.

TOM. Yep.

ADAM. Stay put, let the value increase, release the capital when you have to.

TOM. Yup.

LOUISE. But maybe that's now.

IZZY. Ha-ha!

ADAM. Well, it isn't.

IZZY. I think it's a brilliant plan.

ADAM. Why d'you want to go so much, anyway?

IZZY. I did a month out there last summer –

ADAM. Three weeks, more like two and a half actually –

IZZY. I loved it. Why shouldn't I love it more if I go and do it properly?

ADAM. You don't do anything properly.

IZZY. Piss off.

ADAM. It's true, you never finish things, you flee so you don't have to witness the mess you've made, the pain you've caused, don't have to *think*, you never think –

IZZY. You know what I'm thinking right now?

ADAM. You say it's like being in *The Sound of Music*, great for three weeks, you'll do twenty shows with the von Trapp children, get bored and lonely, have sex with some hapless missionary and come running home.

TOM. How is this helping?

ADAM. My point is Izzy's fleeting desire is not a good enough reason to sell.

TOM. You're a cold fish sometimes.

ADAM. Maybe I just see things clearly.

LOUISE. What is a good enough reason?

ADAM. It's not up to me.

LOUISE. So if I choose to do it –

ADAM. She'll spend her lump sum in three months and won't be able to tell you where it's gone.

IZZY. Hey!

LOUISE. That's her choice, though, isn't it?

ADAM. Well, I've told you what I think.

LOUISE. No. You've deflected the whole discussion onto Izzy and bullied her like a schoolboy. *You* don't want us to leave. Do you?

IZZY. Aha!

LOUISE. Why not?

Silence.

ADAM *puts on his jacket.*

And now you're leaving?

ADAM. Like a schoolboy.

LOUISE *resets her chair.*

ADAM. You don't do anything properly.

IZZY. Piss off.

ADAM. You flee so you don't have to witness the mess you've made, the pain you've caused –

TOM. How would you like it if she did this to you?

ADAM. She wouldn't be saying something I don't already know! (*To* IZZY.) Know thyself! It's not like you're actually stupid, despite only having two GCSEs to your name.

IZZY *bursts into tears.*

LOUISE *moves towards her.*

IZZY. Don't.

They watch IZZY *cry.*

TOM *hands her his handkerchief.*

(*Crying harder.*) Oh, Dad! Your hankie!

TOM. Why do hummingbirds hum?

IZZY (*handing his hankie back*). They don't know the words.

TOM. Yup.

They all look at ADAM.

ADAM. I didn't mean to make you cry.

IZZY. You did.

TOM/LOUISE. Yes.

LOUISE. You do this. Make it all about Izzy. Why don't you
want us to leave?

ADAM *shrugs*.

(*Exasperated*.) Oh!

IZZY *resets her chair*.

ADAM. You don't do anything properly, you flee so you don't
have to witness the mess you've made or –

TOM. How is this helping?

IZZY. No, he's right, I do. I run after people. Away from people.
Just run. Don't I?

LOUISE. Sometimes.

IZZY. But out there you're so far from everything you can't run,
you've got to stay put and see what happens. I'll probably
hate it. But what if I don't?

LOUISE. Yes.

IZZY. Remember the Barcelona suitcase?

LOUISE. Oh!

ADAM (*to* TOM). That was your fault.

IZZY (*to* ADAM). It was your fault.

LOUISE. It was my fault.

ADAM. Coach C, Dad.

TOM. Yep. Izzy, you just get on the train, okay?

LOUISE. Can't she carry the extra one?

TOM. Too heavy.

ADAM. It's coming!

TOM. You do it.

LOUISE. *And* my big one?

ADAM. Coach C, Dad.

TOM. Yep.

IZZY. Whooo!

LOUISE. But it weighs a ton.

ADAM. It's silver!

TOM. I'll take your one and my one, then.

LOUISE. What am I doing?

ADAM. It's D, Dad.

TOM. Take Izzy's.

ADAM. It isn't C!

TOM. Never mind.

ADAM. Now it's E, Dad!

TOM. Just get on.

IZZY. Whooo!

ADAM. Get on E?

TOM. Yep!

LOUISE. Who's doing the extra?

TOM. Izzy, get on.

LOUISE. Tom?

TOM. Ad, bring the extra!

ADAM. Now?

TOM. Just get on the bloody thing.

IZZY. Whooo!

ADAM. It's not C, Dad.

TOM. Never mind!

ADAM. Where's mine?

TOM. Here. Right. Barcelona, here we come.

ADAM. That's not mine.

TOM. What?

LOUISE. Izzy?

ADAM (*tearfully*). It's not my fault! You said bring the extra!

LOUISE. Where's Izzy?

ADAM. Where's mine?

LOUISE. Tom, where's Izzy?

TOM. It's not still on the?

They turn to see IZZY *holding up the suitcase*.

IZZY. I dream about this.

LOUISE/TOM. So do I.

IZZY. You all glide away down the track, I know I'll never
    see you again and the platform turns into like a whirlpool
    and I drown.

TOM. That sort of thing, yup.

IZZY. Sometimes though it's amazing, the train sweeps
    everything clean as it goes and I just belong to somebody else.

ADAM. Who?

TOM. It was the worst.

IZZY. Dad.

TOM. You were five!

LOUISE. You cried on the train.

TOM. Did I?

ADAM. Dad did?

TOM. She was Chloe's age.

IZZY. But the station man gave me a peach and let me sit in his chair. By the time you got back I was totally ready to live with him.

They all laugh.

LOUISE. Would Chloe like frogspawn?

TOM. What?

ADAM. (Pale.)

IZZY. (Tigers.)

LOUISE. (Watchful.)

TOM. (Freckle.)

LOUISE. Then later on she can feed the tadpoles. They're a bit like pets.

IZZY. I love tadpoles.

LOUISE. That's what made me think of it. Shall we get some?

TOM. That'd be nice.

LOUISE *and* TOM *sit.*

SEX

IZZY. What's up with her?

ADAM. I know.

IZZY. She's sort of –

ADAM. Skittish?

IZZY. How come Chloe gets frogspawn?

ADAM. And just coming out with selling like that.

IZZY. You don't want us to leave.

ADAM. I want a ciggie! Not while they're out there. Last time
I did that I caught them at it.

IZZY. *What?*

ADAM. Not actually.

IZZY. Kissing?

ADAM. Hugging. For an absurdly long time.

IZZY. D'you think they're still –

ADAM. Don't even start that sentence.

IZZY *looks at her phone, laughs.*

ADAM *rolls a cigarette.*

What?

IZZY. Just Boyd.

ADAM. Helen's off to Bristol soon.

IZZY. Yeah, how's that going to be?

ADAM *shrugs.*

ADAM. I think it might be the end.

IZZY. You always think that, though.

ADAM. But this is such an obvious moment.

IZZY. For?

ADAM. Her to say you're boring me to death.

IZZY. Did something happen?

ADAM. God, no. If only. If only a giant hand would reach
down through the clouds and tickle us into life. Me, I mean.

IZZY. Is there someone at work who'd tickle you?

ADAM. Tickling in the library? Lawks! You saying I should
have a fling?

IZZY. A good hard flirt. What about that one we had a drink with?

ADAM. Deborah?

IZZY. She was sexy.

ADAM. Like a surgeon's sexy.

IZZY. She has her eye on you.

ADAM. Does she? My God. I'd turn to jelly in front of her and dribble.

IZZY. Babble.

ADAM. And if she has, it's only because she's heard how well-endowed I am.

IZZY. Professor!

ADAM. Yes, in the cranial department, huge. How do you do it?

IZZY. What?

ADAM. Well, you and Boyd have fun, don't you?

IZZY. D'you mean in bed?

ADAM. Oh God.

IZZY. D'you ever try out new things?

ADAM. No.

IZZY. Okay, so –

ADAM. No, I mean, I know you're the Wikipedia of sex, but still.

IZZY. What?

ADAM. You're my sister, I can't talk to you about it!

IZZY. Okay. You didn't used to mind.

ADAM. That was then.

IZZY. Were we weird then?

ADAM. Just a bit. And I didn't tell you my sex things, I just listened to yours.

IZZY. I think mine were like presents.

ADAM (*appalled*). What do you mean?

IZZY. To tempt you down into the world.

ADAM. Oh my God that sounds so. Sad.

IZZY. You were sad.

ADAM. Stoned mostly.

IZZY. Up on the roof, dreaming of Sinead O'Kelly.

ADAM. I touched her shoulder once.

ADAM *lights his spliff.*

They share it, heads close together.

Up on the roof like some fat grey spider, listening to whatever you tell me. Then I go over it all again in private. You know? And I know you're going to get hurt by some shithead at one of these parties. But I never move a muscle. Worse than that.

IZZY. Ad.

ADAM. I'm too scared to do anything myself, so I want you to go further.

IZZY. I want to go further.

ADAM. You're fifteen.

IZZY. I feel like twenty-two. Sex, booze, dysfunctional parents, the queen of cool.

ADAM. You in A & E isn't cool.

IZZY. Oh.

ADAM. Mum'll never forgive me. And why should she?

IZZY. It's nothing to do with you. If I choose to drink a gallon of vodka –

ADAM. I'm at the party!

IZZY. You couldn't have stopped me.

ADAM. But I didn't try.

ADAM *resets his chair*.

ADAM. How do you do it?

IZZY. What?

ADAM. Well, you and Boyd have fun, don't you?

IZZY. D'you mean in bed?

ADAM. Mm.

IZZY. D'you ever try out new things?

ADAM. Um. Sometimes. Rarely. We still don't have fun. Or.

IZZY. Intensity?

ADAM. We don't have intensity.

IZZY. Never? Ad. It's only me.

ADAM. I know. I just can't.

ADAM *resets his chair*.

ADAM. We don't have intensity.

IZZY. Never?

ADAM. Only in my head. In my head I'm bold – adoring, I make her alive with.

IZZY. Excitement.

ADAM. Yes and I think, be that, do that, because I do love her, you know? I think it counts as love. But in our real bed I can't make it happen.

IZZY. Scared to?

ADAM. I can't find the actual feeling.

   IZZY *leans against* ADAM.

   I'm so sick of myself.

IZZY. Sometimes with Boyd –

ADAM. Fuck's sake.

IZZY. Close your eyes or something. Sometimes if we both keep going we just sort of slide into it – intensity. Like when you're swimming, the sea's turquoise turquoise turquoise then suddenly it's dark green and you can't see the bottom. It's only just ahead of you, is what I mean. And Boyd's different there, I don't know him, maybe it's essence of Boyd, and he doesn't know me, either. I love it there.

ADAM. I've never been.

ADAM *opens his eyes.*

She'll leave me, Iz.

They lean against each other.

LOUISE. Will it make Chloe feel sick?

TOM. Oh. Gloopy.

LOUISE. Squelchy.

TOM. She likes jelly, though.

LOUISE. All the little black dots.

TOM. Mm.

LOUISE. All those beginnings.

TOM. You had your hair done?

LOUISE. What?

TOM. Something.

LOUISE *laughs.*

Have you?

LOUISE. No.

TOM. Well, there's definitely something.

LOUISE. I've been eating lots of carrots lately.

TOM. That'll be it. Put hairs on your chest.

LOUISE. I hope not.

TOM. Make it curl, I mean.

LOUISE. Carrots make you see in the dark, don't they?

TOM. That's beans.

LOUISE. They just make you fart like a horse.

They laugh.

TOM. These little curls round your ears.

LOUISE. Which?

TOM. They new?

LOUISE. I don't think so.

TOM. These.

TOM *touches* LOUISE*'s hair.*

Pretty.

LOUISE. Thanks.

They look at each other.

What?

TOM. I like looking at you.

LOUISE. Do you?

TOM. Yep.

They smile.

Is this allowed?

LOUISE. I don't know.

TOM. Probably not.

LOUISE. No.

TOM. I don't quite know where we are.

LOUISE. You never do.

TOM. Okay. Sorry.

LOUISE. No, I don't mean –

TOM. Shall we go back?

LOUISE. No, I didn't mean – I meant it's just so weird how we're all these things at the same time, you know, they don't quite go away ever, they just hang there quietly inside us and wait, in case they're called up again, so you can be everything you ever were *and* the thing now that's different, all at the same time, you know?

She laughs.

I just mean, a life is such a strange thing. Isn't it?

TOM *smiles.*

LOUISE *and* TOM *stand.*

TOM. Seen the frogs? They're actually leaping.

LOUISE. It's an orgy out there.

TOM. Though there's one with no back legs, he's a bit unhoppy.

IZZY/TOM. Ha-ha.

LOUISE. And there's one half-asleep on the compost heap.

ADAM. Rhymes.

IZZY. He jumps in the pond and behind a little green frond he meets –

LOUISE. A blonde. It's always a blonde.

TOM. Ribbit.

They all laugh.

ADAM. They all know it's spring, so they start to sing –

IZZY/LOUISE. Ribbit, ribbit, ribbit!

IZZY. And they're singing while they're swinging –

ADAM. They set to with a leap –

LOUISE. They don't bother to sleep –

IZZY. Till the sun gets warm and the pond fills up with spawn –

LOUISE. Which we put in a jar –

TOM. In the boot of my car –

IZZY. All thick and wobbly –

LOUISE/ADAM. Wobbly?

IZZY. Sorry!

LOUISE. Um.

ADAM. Which Chloe will love prob'ly!

IZZY. Good save, professor.

LOUISE. Or so wobbly and thick it'll make her feel –

ALL. Sick!

General cheers.

ADAM. See, Dad, poetry can be useful.

TOM. Yeah?

ADAM. It cheers you up.

LOUISE. Oh Mr Wordsworth, what magnificent couplets! I love the way they bounce!

ADAM (*Northern*). Would you like to see my pathetic fallacy?

TOM. Your what?

LOUISE. My God, Ad, what will we do with all your books if we move? I mean hundreds and hundreds and hundreds of them.

ADAM *looks at her.*

What?

ADAM *resets his chair.*

TOM *and* LOUISE *sit.*

ADAM. I want a ciggie! Not while they're out there. Last time I did that I caught them at it.

IZZY. *What?*

ADAM. Not actually.

IZZY. Kissing?

ADAM. Hugging. For an absurdly long time.

IZZY. D'you think they're still –

ADAM. No! And anyway, what difference does it make *what* they feel, when there's Sheena and Chloe and another one on the way?

IZZY. Don't you ever wonder?

ADAM. No.

IZZY. I do. I bet they do. Cos it was definitely a possibility.

ADAM. You used to say this when you were stoned. Over and over.

IZZY. Because it was! He'd left Sheena, he was living in that weird bedsit, every time I bunked off school I'd find him here – it was happening.

ADAM. When she was making the pond, you mean?

IZZY. Yeah.

ADAM. No.

IZZY. We watched them from the roof.

ADAM. I know. But that isn't what we saw.

IZZY. You're kidding me.

ADAM. Go on then. What did we see?

TOM *and* LOUISE *stand.*

LOUISE *gets a white cloth out of the suitcase.*

IZZY. She digs for ages. She throws earth over her shoulder, it falls on his shoes.

ADAM. She won't let him help.

TOM *and* LOUISE *unfold the cloth and cover the table.*

IZZY (*as they do this*). She lets him carry the lining with her.

ADAM. Well, it's too heavy for one.

LOUISE *brings four bowls one by one from the suitcase and sets them.*

(*As she does this*.) She brings big stones, she goes to and fro with them, to weigh the lining down. He isn't allowed to touch them, is he?

IZZY. No. It's her thing.

ADAM. He's not allowed to talk, either.

IZZY. He doesn't know what to say.

ADAM. She talks. On and on and on. She's so angry.

IZZY. She's so hurt.

ADAM. He keeps coming back, though.

IZZY. She draws him back.

ADAM. Yeah.

IZZY. Every Monday he's there.

ADAM. Starting to hope.

IZZY. So's she.

ADAM. She's got other ideas.

IZZY. What d'you mean?

ADAM. She tucks her dress into her knickers to wade into the deep bit. He can't take his eyes off her.

IZZY. You can't see that from the roof! Not with your speccy eyes you can't.

TOM *brings* LOUISE *four spoons and she sets them.*

ADAM (*as they do this*). He takes off his shoes and socks –

IZZY. It's to pass her the plants she wants.

TOM/LOUISE. Lilies.

IZZY. And that weird one –

LOUISE. Bogbean.

ADAM. He stands in the shallow bit, trousers rolled up, looking stupid. He's hooked.

LOUISE *and* TOM *put their chairs side by side and sit.*

IZZY (*as they do*). They sit side by side when it's finished. Not talking.

ADAM. Waiting.

IZZY. For what?

ADAM. Forgiveness. And then?

IZZY. It stops.

ADAM. Yeah.

IZZY. They just stop meeting.

ADAM. Why?

IZZY. I don't know.

ADAM. She's filled him from tip to toe with hope.

IZZY. So?

ADAM. So she can crush him.

IZZY. What?

ADAM. It doesn't get more painful than that. She wants him to know that.

IZZY. No.

ADAM. Vengeance is mine.

IZZY. No, no. No!

ADAM. Then why do they just stop?

ADAM *packs the spoons and bowls into the suitcase.*

She pulverises him, then she shuts up shop.

IZZY. And he goes back to Sheena.

ADAM. (Tough.)

IZZY. (Hips.)

ADAM. (Microwave meals.)

IZZY. No, you're wrong. Mum was hopeful, too.

ADAM. To lead him on.

IZZY. What?

ADAM. Why else does it all just stop?

LOUISE *and* TOM *stand.*

TOM. Seen the frogs? There's one in open-toad sandals.

LOUISE. Ribbit.

They both laugh.

TOM. So. Izzy.

IZZY. What?

TOM. Your project.

IZZY. Oh.

TOM. I've looked at the finances again. I'd like to help.

IZZY. Wow.

TOM. Yep. It's going to be tight, but count me in.

IZZY. Wow.

TOM. Yep. (*To* LOUISE.) So there's no need for you to move.

IZZY. Dad, that's brilliant.

TOM. I always want to help with your things, you know that.

LOUISE. But you're still moving?

TOM. It's not a problem.

LOUISE. I thought that was taking up all the slack.

TOM. We're not moving, okay?

LOUISE. Right. You'll all manage in the flat?

TOM. Yup. So –

LOUISE. It's Sheena. Isn't it?

IZZY. Is it?

LOUISE. Tom. When?

IZZY. Oh Dad.

TOM. Thursday night. We got to the hospital and they tried but.

LOUISE. How is she?

TOM *shakes his head.*

TOM. So. Anyway. I'd like to help you go and do your thing.

IZZY. Oh no!

TOM. Don't.

IZZY. Sorry. Just. It's all so.

IZZY *cries.*

TOM *hands her his handkerchief.*

(*Crying harder.*) Not your hankie!

TOM. For God's sake.

ADAM. Will you stop?

IZZY. I'm trying!

ADAM. Such a dick.

LOUISE. Adam.

IZZY *blows her nose and hands* TOM *his handkerchief.*

I'm so sorry.

ADAM. Yeah.

TOM. *Enough!*

Silence.

So. Given the circumstances. There's really no need for you to up sticks here.

ADAM. No.

TOM. No.

LOUISE. No.

LOUISE *and* TOM *take the tablecloth and billow it between them.*

ADAM *runs underneath the cloth.*

ADAM (*laughing*). Again!

They billow it between them.

ADAM *runs underneath the cloth.*

IZZY *lies on the table.*

(*Laughing.*) Again!

They billow the cloth and bring it down over IZZY *like a sheet.*

They gather round her.

IZZY *lies completely still, her eyes closed.*

LOUISE. (Small.)

TOM. (White.)

LOUISE. (Still.)

TOM. (Mine.)

IZZY (*eyes closed, quietly*). It's nothing to do with you.

ADAM *crawls up the table towards her.*

(*Eyes closed, quietly.*) If I choose to drink a gallon of vodka –

ADAM. I'm at the party.

LOUISE. (Hands.)

TOM. (Still.)

LOUISE. (Mine.)

TOM *can't bear to look, turns away.*

IZZY (*eyes closed*). You couldn't have stopped me.

ADAM *rests his head on* IZZY*'s hip.*

ADAM. But I didn't try.

He gets off the table and rolls a cigarette.

LOUISE *folds up the cloth and puts it in the suitcase.*

TOM, LOUISE *and* IZZY *polish.*

MOVING

IZZY. Knock knock.

TOM. Who's there?

IZZY. Little old lady.

TOM. Little old lady who?

IZZY. I didn't know you could yodel.

TOM/IZZY. Ha-ha.

LOUISE. Only.

ADAM. What?

LOUISE. Since I started thinking about it.

ADAM. Dad's plan is better.

LOUISE. Maybe.

ADAM. You'd have a lot more options.

TOM. Yup.

LOUISE. Mm.

ADAM. What?

LOUISE. I think I've got used to the idea. Of moving.

IZZY. You're in such a funny mood.

LOUISE. Am I?

IZZY. Next you're going to say you're seeing someone.

LOUISE. Actually.

IZZY *gasps.*

Silence.

ADAM, IZZY *and* TOM *talk to themselves, at the same time, but in their own rhythm:*

ADAM. just walking away as if there weren't casualties, life-changing injuries, you are not, there are things, no things are not no

IZZY. a colt on long long legs and she can't stop running in a great green field and now there's, who is he? oh go Mum, go faster, go faster

TOM. not too fast, too fast, I don't want I want I don't know but I don't want it to go like this so fast, and what will I?

Silence.

LOUISE *laughs.*

LOUISE. Your faces.

IZZY. Who?

LOUISE. No one!

IZZY. Mum.

LOUISE. But you never know.

IZZY. Excellent.

ADAM. Which bit?

IZZY. All of it, moving, finding a new someone. Isn't it?

LOUISE. I want to be – you know, lighter.

IZZY. Yes!

ADAM. Why is it you who gets to be lighter?

LOUISE. How d'you mean?

ADAM. Well, I'd love to be lighter, fat fucking chance, and whose fault is that?

TOM. Gently.

LOUISE. You're angry with me.

ADAM. You think?

LOUISE. Why?

ADAM. You broke Izzy's heart, you do know that?

IZZY. Not broke it, no.

ADAM. You had a choice.

IZZY. Dad started it.

ADAM. But she could've had him back, could've held us together like it mattered, she preferred revenge, okay, but so she doesn't get to wriggle free now and leave us here, she has to live in the fucking icebox, too.

LOUISE. It wasn't –

ADAM. To be lighter is my fantasy.

LOUISE. Maybe it's everyone's –

ADAM. In reality I live in a library with the other speccy men, we're going to write obscure books and smell of fags and wank frantically in our single college beds and during the night bookworms will bore through our eyes, so the only useful parts of us will disintegrate at a knock.

LOUISE. That's horrible, what is that? self-pity.

ADAM. Alright. Here's a cooler assessment of your impact: this man shouldn't be teaching love poetry. It's like asking a halibut to understand a panther.

He picks up his jacket.

LOUISE. Don't you dare, Adam.

ADAM. I've already said too much. It won't get us anywhere, it's just words, endless words.

ADAM *leaves.*

LOUISE *resets her chair.*

LOUISE. You're angry with me.

ADAM. You think?

LOUISE. Why?

ADAM *leaves.*

(*Shouts.*) Oh!

IZZY *resets her chair.*

LOUISE. You're angry with me.

ADAM. It's just words, endless –

IZZY. You love words!

> LOUISE *puts on* ADAM*'s jacket and zips it up.*

ADAM. That is so fucking childish.

> LOUISE *shrugs.*

Give me my jacket, please. I want to leave.

> LOUISE *shrugs.*

Is that me, you being me?

> ADAM *chases* LOUISE.

(*Running.*) Such a hypocrite, telling us to be kind, you weren't kind.

> ADAM *catches her.*

We were there, too! Or did you forget? We had to go through it all again and it's worse the second time, sick with hope.

LOUISE. When was this?

ADAM. If you'd just shut up and held his hands. But you talked.

LOUISE. How do you know this?

IZZY. We watched you.

ADAM. On and on and on, you stupid bitch.

TOM. Hey!

ADAM. Then we have to stand in Dad's grotesque teenage bedsit while he tells us you won't have him back, and feel the layers of that hardening inside.

IZZY. It's not Mum's fault you're shut up like a snail.

ADAM. You mean a clam.

IZZY. A clam then, a clam!

ADAM. A cold fish, a numb fuck who never thaws out, a big
   brain wobbling on a little cold body like Humpty fucking
   Dumpty: you did that. You picked up a hammer and smacked
   the eggs to smithereens.

TOM. That's not fair!

ADAM. Smack smack smack.

TOM. No! That's not how it went.

ADAM. And now we have to be kind cos finally you want to
   open your thighs to some poor prick – you must be so dry by
   now, will he get inside you? I hope it's a wretched sore fuck.

   IZZY sits.

   ADAM sits.

IZZY. Go away.

ADAM. Oh God.

IZZY. Get away from me.

ADAM. Iz?

IZZY. Get away.

LOUISE. I'm alright.

TOM. You're not.

LOUISE. He has to say things.

TOM. Not those.

   IZZY stands.

   ADAM stands.

IZZY (*to* ADAM). Don't you speak to her. Get out of here, get
   out!

   ADAM sits.

   Mum.

   IZZY hugs LOUISE.

   I'm so sorry.

ADAM *tries to roll a cigarette.*

TOM *sits.*

TOM. I started it. Why not say things to me?

ADAM. Shit.

He gives up with the cigarette.

Could you go away, please?

TOM. That's not how it went.

ADAM. Please?

TOM. She never stopped thinking about you, never. She never
does.

TOM *stands.*

ADAM *stands.*

IZZY. Get out!

ADAM. What did happen then?

TOM. What?

ADAM. If that's not how it went. Dad?

TOM *puts the lid on the wax.*

You just said it. That's not how it went. So what did happen?

IZZY. Dad?

TOM *folds his polishing cloth up small.*

Silence.

TOM (*quietly to* LOUISE). Why don't you tell them?

TOM *sits.*

IZZY. Mum?

LOUISE. No.

IZZY. What?

LOUISE. No.

IZZY. But we have a right to know.

LOUISE. A right?

IZZY. Okay, not a right. We need to know. Do we need to know?

LOUISE. They're Dad's things. So you should hear them from him.

IZZY. Look at him! And what if he never says?

LOUISE. Then he never does.

IZZY. Tell us! Why won't you say?

ADAM. She's protecting him. Or us.

LOUISE. You hungry?

IZZY. Tell us.

LOUISE. Adam?

ADAM *shakes his head.*

LOUISE *puts the cloth on the table.*

I invited you to lunch. Come on, we must all be starving by now. Tom!

TOM *stands.*

There's soup.

IZZY (*to* TOM). Your face.

TOM. What?

IZZY. She hasn't said a word.

TOM. Right.

LOUISE. Soup and bread. I hope that's okay.

IZZY. I see how it went.

LOUISE. Do you?

IZZY (*to* TOM). When Boyd says I can't do this, I want us to be *one* and not have other people, I agree cos I love him and the simplest thing is not to tell him, in some ways it's better, when other people are forbidden it's more exciting and the sex is better, and then when Boyd finds out, which he always does, and never from me, he sits and sobs and I have to watch him and I hate myself, you know, well yes, you must know, but it doesn't stop me doing it again because I'm sorry but not sorry enough, kind but not kind enough, just a miserable human-size amount, till the day comes Boyd wakes up and thinks there isn't enough glue to put us together, even though I'll beg him and feel my best life running out of my hands. You know?

TOM *hands* LOUISE *the bowls, which she sets one by one.*

He hands her the spoons, which she sets.

(*As they do this.*) You stood there, while Mum made the pond, waiting to be forgiven, and you found that Mum was filling up with hope and suddenly you were, too, only you'd lied about Sheena. You promised Mum it was finished, you promised us it was, but you couldn't quite give her up, it was too compelling. So all the time Mum was doing the pond you knew she was going to find out you were lying, and it just made you want to come home all the more.

ADAM (*to* TOM). Is this right?

IZZY. And when she finds out, her face is just like Boyd's, that you've lied *again*, broken trust *again*, she feels sick and wobbly. Just hasn't got it in her to try again. Because we are incorrigible. No words for that.

Silence.

TOM. You know. She's never broken the thread. She's always let it run.

EAT

LOUISE. We should eat.

TOM. I'll go.

IZZY. Go on, then.

TOM. If that's what you want.

IZZY. Don't hang about here for scraps.

LOUISE. Izzy.

IZZY. What? I don't want to sit down with him. With either of them.

LOUISE. No.

IZZY. Why go on with it, then?

LOUISE. Because if we go on, I think –

IZZY. Making people be nice to each other when what they actually feel.

TOM. Say it.

IZZY. Just go away.

TOM. Yep.

LOUISE (*to* TOM). Soup first.

IZZY. *I'll* go, then.

    IZZY *leaves*.

TOM. I'll give you a ring, Louise.

LOUISE. Okay.

TOM. Adam.

    ADAM *doesn't look at* TOM.

TOM *leaves*.

LOUISE. You'll have some soup.

ADAM. I must run.

LOUISE. Roll me a ciggie first.

ADAM *rolls a cigarette*.

D'you think she's gone to Boyd's?

ADAM. Probably.

LOUISE. I hate that way she talks about herself. Let's smoke in here, keep warm.

ADAM. Don't.

LOUISE. What?

ADAM. Make things easy for me.

LOUISE. I'm not, I'm –

ADAM. Please.

He holds out the roll-up.

LOUISE. We don't have to leave.

ADAM. What?

LOUISE. If you're not ready.

ADAM. No –

LOUISE. We'll –

ADAM. Don't, it isn't – it's not – please, I can't –

ADAM *leaves*.

LOUISE. Oh fuck.

LOUISE *resets her chair*.

LOUISE. We should eat.

ADAM. I'll go.

IZZY. Go on, then.

LOUISE. Izzy.

IZZY. What? I don't want to sit down with him, with either of them.

LOUISE. No.

IZZY. If he thinks it's alright to talk to you in that foul way –

ADAM. I don't.

IZZY. You disgust me. I don't want to see you again. I mean it, Adam.

LOUISE. You don't, so don't say it.

IZZY. You said you'd leave.

ADAM. Can I say something first?

IZZY. No.

ADAM. Iz.

IZZY. I don't want to hear it!

LOUISE. We'll be outside.

TOM *and* LOUISE *sit*.

ADAM. I'm sorry. So sorry.

IZZY. It's Mum you should be telling.

ADAM. I can't yet.

IZZY. Is that it?

ADAM. I don't know what else to say.

IZZY. Piss off then.

ADAM. Isobel.

IZZY. All that rubbish boiling inside you, pouring it over Mum
so *you* don't have to get hurt, all this time you blame her and
blame her and now you go and hurt her more, it's vicious.
I've always wanted to be like you, *be* you, you seemed so
big and wise, but you're mean and *small*.

ADAM *nods*.

Go away then and stay away.

IZZY *goes under the table*.

ADAM *crouches near*.

ADAM. Please don't say you won't see me again.

IZZY. I won't.

ADAM. I've offended you. Deeply. I know that. Let alone
Mum. But say you'll see me one day.

IZZY. No.

ADAM. Iz! Just one day.

IZZY. No.

ADAM. We belong to each other. Don't make me do it on my
own.

He curls up against a table leg.

LOUISE *stands and watches them, but neither moves*.

LOUISE *resets her chair*.

LOUISE. We should eat.

ADAM/TOM. I'll go.

LOUISE. No.

IZZY. *I'll* go, then.

LOUISE. Want to do something for me, Izzy?

IZZY. What?

LOUISE. Do you?

IZZY. I s'pose so. Yeah.

> LOUISE *gets a thermos from the suitcase, hands it to* IZZY.

> Is it home-made?

> IZZY *opens it.*

> *They gather.*

ADAM. It's chicken, isn't it?

TOM. Smells amazing.

> LOUISE *gets a baguette from the suitcase.*

LOUISE. All this mortifying knowledge hanging in the air. But we are bodies. And I think it would be kind.

IZZY. Mum –

LOUISE. Difficult. Very. Not enjoyable. Kind.

> LOUISE *sits at the table.*

> You probably have to practise it.

> LOUISE *pours soup into four bowls.*

> *She tears the bread into four.*

> IZZY *sits.*

> *Then* TOM *sits.*

> *Then* ADAM *sits.*

> *They taste the soup.*

IZZY. Yum.

TOM/ADAM. Mm.

LOUISE. Not bad.

> *They eat.*

> I finished the cheese last night I'm ever so sorry since the redundancy I just garden all day and when I stop I'm ravenous so I had a cheese omelette and now there's only soup and bread I'm so –

IZZY. Mum.

TOM. It's delicious.

ADAM *nods*.

They eat.

How do you handle a dangerous cheese?

IZZY. Caerphilly.

TOM. Yup.

They eat.

LOUISE. So d'you think Boyd might help us?

IZZY. Sell? But he'll flirt with you terribly, it's his secret weapon.

LOUISE. Is it?

IZZY. There's a scoreboard in the office, he's often number one.

LOUISE. Is he?

IZZY. There's a book of the weird things people do when
    they're shown round, too.

LOUISE. Go on.

IZZY. So one woman went round trying all the beds, like
    Goldilocks, they had to say you know they won't be staying?
    And one couple, Boyd was talking to the wife, the husband
    went off, they found him having a shower, he was naked, he
    said he was testing the water pressure.

They all laugh.

They eat.

LOUISE. Do they ever get propositioned?

IZZY. Boyd's had it twice. It's when the house is empty.

ADAM. Honestly?

LOUISE. I can understand that. Well, Boyd's very attractive.

IZZY. I'm telling him you said that. He'll never stop hugging
    that to himself.

LOUISE. Why?

IZZY. You're his fantasy woman.

LOUISE. Don't be daft.

IZZY. Ever since school! Intelligent, kind, lovely to look at, what else d'you want? That's what he says.

LOUISE. Moving swiftly on.

ADAM. What did Boyd do?

IZZY. When?

ADAM. When he was propositioned.

IZZY. The first time he was so stunned he just bundled her into the car, but the second time.

ADAM. Kidding me.

IZZY. First he said he went for it, then he said he didn't. What d'you think?

ADAM. No way.

IZZY. I think he just wanted to add to his mystery.

ADAM. Boyd doesn't have any, that's why we love him.

LOUISE. He's the straightest person I know.

ADAM. Upright.

LOUISE. Yes, upright.

They eat.

TOM. Sometimes I get this thing like a daydream. It's usually when I'm working. I'm on a boat out at sea and you're on the beach, you three, making a sandcastle, you're not children, you're grown up, I can't get in to the shore, the wind's driving me out, I can't even get your attention, I can just see you there together. It's terrible.

Silence.

LOUISE, IZZY *and* ADAM *talk to themselves, at the same time, but in their own rhythm:*

LOUISE. so we are still one thing somehow, you never said that before, a unit, a bundle, in some part of your mind still together in some part of you

IZZY. all there will ever be is this sidling up to the fence, shuffling up sideways, squinting and huffing and panicking backwards again and not quite getting over

ADAM. you and me, you and me both, outwardly solid steady capable, inwardly panic-stricken incoherent unravelling terrified boobies

Silence.

IZZY. You're always fixing things.

TOM. What?

IZZY. Yeah. You're always under the sink or soldering something outside the back door or up some ladder Mum's scared of, cleaning the gutters. You must get *some* points for that.

TOM. I'll take any points.

IZZY. You need 'em.

TOM. Yep.

IZZY. I'm going to get the ten past. Mum, I'll talk to Boyd.

IZZY hugs LOUISE.

LOUISE. Sweet girl.

IZZY (*to* ADAM). You getting the train?

LOUISE. Yes.

ADAM (*to* LOUISE). Am I?

LOUISE. Yes. I'll see you soon.

ADAM puts on his jacket, pockets the book.

IZZY and ADAM leave.

LOUISE sits down and cries.

TOM draws close.

It's so hard to be kind to them when they're so.

TOM. What?

LOUISE. Horrible. He hurts me.

TOM. Yep.

LOUISE. He hates me.

TOM. No.

LOUISE. He's locked inside himself and I can't bear it.

   TOM *finds a clean section of his hankie for her.*

   She blows and hands it back.

   It's like trying to conduct the sea.

TOM. What is?

   LOUISE *gathers bowls, spoons and packs them.*

   TOM *packs the thermos.*

   They fold the cloth together.

   LOUISE *packs it and fastens the suitcase.*

LOUISE. Would you like to have the table?

TOM. It's yours.

LOUISE. You made it.

TOM. Don't you want it?

LOUISE. I might not have room.

TOM. Well, we certainly don't.

LOUISE. I'm just being –

TOM. Hard-nosed?

LOUISE. Practical.

TOM. Do what you want with it.

   They carry the table.

LOUISE (*as they do*). (Homework.)

TOM. (Hiding.)

LOUISE. (Alphabetti Spaghetti.)

TOM. (Chisel.)

LOUISE. You sure?

TOM. I s'pose it might squeeze in somewhere.

They carry the table off and come back.

LOUISE. God, I'm exhausted. Are you?

TOM. Yep.

LOUISE. And you get up early.

TOM. Chloe's always so cheerful first thing I don't really mind. She loves the tadpoles. She mothers them.

LOUISE. Good.

LOUISE *picks up the suitcase.*

They look at each other.

You could at least be happy for me.

TOM. I'm trying.

LOUISE. Okay. I'll just put this –

TOM. Yep.

LOUISE. You coming?

TOM. Right behind you.

LOUISE *leaves.*

TOM *looks round the house.*

He sits down.

End.

www.nickhernbooks.co.uk

facebook.com/nickhernbooks

twitter.com/nickhernbooks